Our One-Way Street

Also by Rebecca Schumejda

Full-length Poetry Books

Waiting at the Dead End Diner (Bottom Dog Press, 2014)
Cadillac Men (NYQ Books, 2012)
Falling Forward (sunnyoutside, 2009)

Chapbooks

Common Wages (with Don Winter, Working Stiff Press, 2017)
From Seed to Sin (Bottle of Smoke Press, 2011)
The Map of Our Garden (verve bath, 2009)
Dream Big Work Harder (sunnyoutside press 2006)
The Tear Duct of the Storm (Green Bean Press, 2001)

Our One-Way Street

Poems by

Rebecca Schumejda

NY Books™

The New York Quarterly Foundation, Inc.
New York, New York

NYQ Books™ is an imprint of The New York Quarterly Foundation, Inc.

The New York Quarterly Foundation, Inc.
P. O. Box 2015
Old Chelsea Station
New York, NY 10113

www.nyq.org

First Edition

Set in New Baskerville

Layout and Design by Raymond P. Hammond

Proof Editing by Kimberly Boland

Cover Art: "Strange Days," Photograph by Alexis Rhone Fancher, 2016
www.alexisrhonefancher.com

Author Photograph by Kaya Lanier

Library of Congress Control Number: 2017948474

ISBN: 978-1-63045-045-8

Our One-Way Street

Acknowledgments

Some of these pieces have appeared in *Arsenic Lobster, A Slant of Light: An Anthology of Hudson Valley Women Writers, Big Hammer, Chiron Review, Every Day Zine, Fried Chicken and Coffee, Hobo Camp Review, The Inflectionist Review Anthology of Poetry, JMWW, The Más Tequila Review, Malpais Review, Misfit Magazine, pemmican, Pif Magazine, Rattle, Ristau: A Journal of Being, Silver Birch Press, Stirring, Tears in the Fence, Up the Staircase Quarterly, Wordsdance.*

"How to Paint in the Dark" appears in the chapbook *Common Wages* co-authored with Don Winter.

With much gratitude to Lei Issacs, my neighbor and fellow poet, one of the unorthodox characters who inspires me to consider the world from a nonsectarian perspective. Also with great respect to the Hudson Valley poetry community.

Contents

Section 2: Stop

Section 3: Dead End

For

John Dorsey and Annie Menenbroker (1936 – 2016)

Section 1: One-Way

How to Classify a Reptile

At the reptile show, I am reminded of him,
the first guy who made me orgasm.
As the presenter drapes a yellow Burmese Python
around his shoulders, I think about how my ex showed up
at my doorstep unannounced over a decade after he said
that I was like his Volvo, comfortable and dependable,
but not worth going back to once he'd driven a sports car.
Yes, he really said that and I said nothing, nothing at all.
Instead, I cried every time I saw his new girlfriend,
his beautiful blonde Ferrari, everywhere I went around campus:
in the food court, at the library, throwing bread to the fish
that swam in the gunky water, playing the bongos outside the art studios,
and smoking clove cigarettes outside the Humanities Building.

While the presenter flips the python over so we can see
the snake's claws, proof of evolutionary progress,
I think about how I let my ex in, how he sat at my kitchen table
while I peeled and sliced an apple for his daughter
and gave her a glass of milk with a red and white striped straw.
I listened as he told me his sob story about his custody battle,
about not having a job, living in his mother's cramped apartment
that didn't even have a bathtub. He even had to wear his bathing suit
to take showers with his daughter. Then he asked me if I had a tub.
I listened and poured him coffee. I made peanut butter and jelly
sandwiches for them while balancing my own infant daughter on my hip.
I did not offer up news about myself; I did not offer up our tub.

I listen as the presenter introduces Ally, a seven-month-old alligator
that the police took away from some guy who was keeping it
as a pet in his bathtub. This happens too much, the presenter says,
then goes on to say that a male can end up weighing up to
eight hundred pounds. He walks around the room to give the kids
a closer look. He explains how, like a submarine,
even when submerged under water, the alligator's periscope-like eyes
allow them to hunt for prey and I look away as Ally blinks at me
and think about how before leaving that day, my ex asked me for
gas money, and without hesitation, I reached into my pocketbook
and gave him all that I had: a ten, a five and three ones.

Our One-Way Street

We let our children ride their bikes on our one-way street at dusk
while we sit on dilapidated porches, discussing how our houses
are worth half of what we paid for them and make bets on whose
roof will go first. We all planned to fix them up, but found out
money is the only thing that leaves this neighborhood fast.
Out of the road! we yell when we see headlights.

I run into the street each time to make sure drivers slow down.
My neighbor to the right, Terry, tells me for the twentieth time
how, while on a bike, he was hit by a car when he was my kid's age,
rolled right over the hood, got back up and rode home.
Look, he says, holding up his hand, wiggling four fingers, *I'm fine.*

Patti, from across the street, donning a raggedy pink bathrobe,
asks, *Did you really go to graduate school?* with the same tone
you'd ask a coworker if they're banging the boss. Shying away
from a response, I go inside to get a box of ice pops. Wine and
beer in big, red, plastic cups appear in our hands. Someone brings
out yesterday's newspaper to show us an article about another
neighbor, busted for growing pot plants in his backyard.

It is too dark for the kids to see the chalk borders I drew
on asphalt earlier and we are buzzed, so the kids take advantage,
moving further and further away from us. Their expanding
ellipses make me feel guilty about accepting another cup of beer.

Crazy Kay, the old lady who lives closest to the dead end sign,
strolls by with two of her stinky, old dogs, stops in the street,
screeches, *Who started the party without me?*
As our kids circle around her, she complains about parking tickets
and the growing number of sinkholes in this city, *If I didn't know
better, I would say that this city is trying to swallow us whole.*

Breaking Free

After the crash, I look out our bedroom window
and spot Mary's teenage granddaughter, Nina,
descending, head first, from her bedroom window.
She is trying to reach an overturned aluminum trash can
with her hands, possibly to move it closer,
but instead she falls and, as if a deranged ninja gymnast,
rolls over the can. Patti's porch lights go on
then the slits of her blinds open. Dogs bark. Nina gets up,
runs into her backyard where she'll undoubtedly jump
the fence, hopefully executing a more graceful dismount.

I envy the thrill of breaking free, the way I did as a teen,
the strategical planning: placing pillows beneath blankets
just in case my parents peeked in; opening the door an
inch at a time while listening for stirring.
Then once away from the house, looking back
from a distance to make sure the lights were still off.
Now back in bed beside my snoring husband,
I open my book to where I left off, but instead of
reading I think about being fifteen, sneaking out to meet
that twenty-three-year-old Korean hunk, who wore
a studded motorcycle jacket, and drove a crotch rocket;
how before speeding down back roads in the early
morning hours, smelling of beer and cigarettes, he took
his helmet off and made me wear it, how for that gesture
I deemed him chivalrous and worth the risk.

Texting in the '80s

In the middle school cafeteria,
Terry's best friend dared him
to throw tatter tots at a table of girls
and he hit Chrissy in the back.
She retaliated by walking over and pouring
her chocolate milk over his mullet.
In lunch detention, the next day,
Terry folded a note that read:
Can I get your number?
into a paper football and flicked it
at the back of Chrissy's head.
The rest is history.

P.S. Terry's best friend ended up being the best man at their
wedding. At the reception, he dared Terry to throw a cocktail
shrimp at Chrissy's back for old times' sake.

A Brief History of a Wind Chime

Restless in bed, past midnight, I listen
to a train in the distance,
to a group of teens walking by
talking about *Oh no, she didn't,*
and to the clanking of wind chimes
on Mary's porch.
I can't sleep, so I concentrate
on those wind chimes,
how they remind me of the time
I found Mary's cat run over in the street,
how it was almost dead,
how I had to tell her.
She didn't know what to do,
so I picked its stiff body up
in my sweatshirt and carried it
to her porch where we watched it die
and then we just sat there for a long time
in silence while Mary pet the cat.
Everything was quiet, except those wind chimes,
until Mary told me about how
she got fired from the nursing home
the day before, for allegedly stealing
a gold cross necklace from one of the residents.
Fifteen years and my supervisor sat me down
and said, "Mary, I know you didn't do this,
but her son plays golf with the director
and well, there's nothing more I can do."

Baseball and Butterflies

Chrissy's four-year-old son
is wearing his snow boots
on a 93 degree day.
She says he refuses to wear
flip flops, sandals or sneakers.
We watch our girls catch butterflies
with cupped hands, while he
swings a wiffle ball bat at anything
moving through air,
and stomps the girls' exposed toes.
Little boys and little girls
are so different, Chrissy chuckles,
just as my daughter holds up
a Monarch caged in her hands
and Chrissy's son swings.

Changing a Tire

Even though my husband told me a dozen times that the fifty mile usage limit is just a suggestion, he finally agrees to change the donut he's been driving on for over three weeks. *You worry too much,* he says on his way out the door.

While jacking up his car, Crazy Kay creeps up and asks if he knows the story of the murderers who lived in our house before we moved in.

Without waiting for his response, she goes on, *In the winter of '01 or maybe '03, well anyway, I helped two young boys push their truck out of your driveway; it was stuck in the snow. When we got it out, they didn't even thank me, just took off. Later, I found out, that very same day, those two boys picked up a prostitute and after a payment dispute, the woman was dragged across a parking lot, ran over and left in a snowbank to die.*

Later my husband tells me how by the time the last bolt was tightened, Crazy Kay was gone, leaving her tale hanging heavy like the humidity in the air. Initially he hid the frayed spare tire, that reinforces how close we live to tragedy, in his trunk, so he didn't have to hear me say, *I told you so.*

Her Slice of Paradise

In her backyard,
Patti created a tropical paradise.
She invites us over
to drink piña coladas
from fancy glasses adorned with
colorful mini-umbrellas
and to admire
her makeshift beach.
We survey sand that
replaced grass,
three plastic coconut trees,
tiki torches,
beach chairs,
beach balls,
shells,
rubber starfish,
and a free-standing hammock
accessorizing her blow up pool.
It is a win-win, Patti says,
pushing up the bridge of her sunglasses,
I get my beach and I don't have to listen
to Henry whine about mowing the lawn.

Career Readiness

While we watch our kids
drawing with chalk on the
cracked sidewalk,
Chrissy confesses
that she only wanted a job
to occupy her time
until she had kids.
In high school, she says,
I took a cosmetology class,
but burnt another student's scalp
while giving her a perm,
so I transferred into the culinary class
and fell in love with baking—
where burning is far less tragic.

The Finelli's House

The Finelli's house,
the second one
to the right of Patti's,
right next to Mary's house,
looks as if it were transplanted
from a better neighborhood
where houses are freshly painted,
yards perfectly manicured,
driveways newly paved.
They don't have last year's
Christmas lights up
like a quarter of our neighbors,
or a dilapidated porch like most,
or cars up on ramps
in the yard.
They aren't involved
with the daily goings-on,
they just happen to be
stuck here
in a house they owe more on
than it's worth.
Their house is the eyesore
on our one-way street,
a reminder of what could be.

Aunt Anne's Cucumbers

From Chrissy's porch,
we watch our kids
play catch with a deflating beach ball
that they found down the street,
in a gutter.
Hey, you want some cucumbers? she asks
and I say, *Sure.*
She goes inside and comes back
with two full plastic bags.

I open one bag and do a quick count,
Wow, there's like fifty here,
where did you get all of these?
I ask, picking one up and studying it.

My great-aunt Anne, she has a big, old,
farm house in Saugerties and after
my uncle passed, she just started growing
cucumbers, nothing but cucumbers.

Why not tomatoes or zucchini? I ask.

Uncle Jim hated cucumbers,
said they were a waste of space, just like her.
So she grows cucumbers, nothing but cucumbers,
and says she thinks of them as hundreds
of middle fingers sticking up at him.

Backyard Mechanics

After Bill's wife left,
he turned his home into
a makeshift boarding house
for his dysfunctional bachelor friends.
His ex-wife's once lavish garden
was transformed into a horseshoe pit.
Her potted plants became
beer can holders and ashtrays.
Her flower beds a resting place
for car parts: old tires, rotted mufflers,
bent rims, broken rearview mirrors
and dented fenders.
Her perennials still peek through their junk:
Purple Phlox, Asters, Peonies
and others with women's names
like Veronnica, Sage, and Iris—
reveal the contrast between how men
and women work through
life's disappointments.

Mowing the Lawn

While I'm mowing the front lawn, Patti marches across the street
waving me down, frantically. When I stop and turn off the mower,
she catches her breath, then says,
I need your opinion on whether or not I went too far this time.
I just found one of those smutty magazines in my mailbox today,
after Henry swore he canceled the subscription. And well, I cut out a picture
of my face, glued it over the cover model's, then added a bubble caption:
"Hey big boy, remember me?" She holds the magazine up, so I can see
   for myself.
After a chuckle, my attention cascades from her statement down to
   the wet grass
stuck to my sneakers and I keep smiling even though I know there
   is a good chance
I won't be able to get this crappy, old push mower started again.

Lacerations

I told you *no, never,*
so when I see
the laceration on the trunk
of the mulberry tree,
the rope and chainsaw
on the lawn,
I know you weren't listening

and if you were,
you didn't remember how
I shivered the first time
your fingers ran along
the scars on my abdomen.

I fear the way shade
abandons a fallen tree
like how love
abandons the disfigured.

Yes, mulberries tracked
into the house stained
the living room carpet,
but I meant it when
I said I will never
take off my shirt,
even if you turn off the lights,
even if the bark heals over.

From Her Kitchen Window

Chrissy and I conduct conversations
through her kitchen window.
Today while I hack the bushes
dividing our yards,
she decorates a three-tier cake
for a friend's wedding.
We chit-chat about our own special days.
Then she confesses, *Terry's barely*
making ends meet, so I am applying
for an overnight baking position.
Noticing how uneven the bushes are,
I laugh, pointing at my handiwork,
Wow, I am really hacking these up.
Chrissy laughs and reciprocates with a story:
Did I tell you about the time when,
before I transferred into culinary,
my high school cosmetology class
went to the local nursing home
to give free haircuts to the residents?

Coffee

One of the only mainstays on Broadway
is Burger King,
where I get my morning coffee.
Somehow the manager, Tony,
always sneaks in the exact number
of days he has left until retirement.
Sometimes the weather is unbearably hot
or wickedly cold,
or his joints are achy or he just got
over a flu, or an employee
failed to show up for a shift
so he had to fill in for them or
a customer was rude or the district manager
is coming in or the corporation is
trying out a new healthy item
that no one wants to order,
but he still has to push
or they have to stay open
an hour later or they have to work
some corny catch phrase into each transaction.
But no matter what is going on,
Tony never fails to remind me
that he is one day closer
to not handing me my morning coffee.

The Fifth Generation

When Terry pulls up,
his kids run to him and he lifts
both of them up into the air at once.
His mother-in-law, who sits on the porch,
lighting a new cigarette for the one
she just finished, shakes her head in disapproval;
she blames him for not maintaining the house
she grew up in. *Five generations of*
laughter, screams and cries bounce off
those plaster walls and now the damn
place is falling apart, she says, picking up
a rusty nail and showing it to me.
My grandmother's and great uncle's height charts
are still visible on the inside of the cellar door.
Terry swings his kids around and around
as they giggle and kick.
You know Beck, she says to me,
when we were kids, we were sent out to play
until it was lunch time and my mom
rang that old rusty cowbell
hanging on the wall in there.
Before we even swallowed the last
of our sandwiches, we were sent right back out
until she rang that bell for dinner.
No one worried about what could happen then.
Heck, we'd ride our bikes without helmets
all over the neighborhood.
She shakes her head,
takes a drag from her cigarette,
looks at the nail in her hand and sighs,
Now everything is falling apart.

Where My Garden Was

Where my small garden was, there is a patch of mud that the neighborhood kids play in. Patti sits on a lawn chair in a floral moo-moo, cooling herself with a plastic spray bottle while her grandson throws mud balls at the other kids. *Why didn't you do the garden this year?* she asks. I shake my head and admit, *Because I want to spend more time fixing up the house, so we can move out of here.* Patti smirks when her grandson tosses a mud ball over my head. Then she halfheartedly scolds him. *Why don't you have a mud pie contest?* I suggest.

I used to have a garden back when I was young like you, Patti says, *it just got to be too much work. I mean, you can get vegetables cheap now at Walmart. I got a bunch of broccoli for fifty-seven cents the other day, fifty-seven cents, you can't beat that,* she says. *Bill's wife, you know the Ukranian woman, she used to have a garden every year, grew the most beautiful produce I have ever seen. Now that she is gone all that man lives on is fast food and beer. Somehow he lost weight. How does that happen?*

The kids use pails as cake molds. *You know they sell drugs at that house now, Bill's house, one of those guys is selling drugs, I know it, all those cars coming and going, waiting out there in the middle of the night. They're getting bold too, blaring music and beeping their horns. I am not saying Bill is selling, but one of those guys is. I have been writing down every license plate. Henry tells me to mind my own business, but this is our neighborhood, honey, even though you think you are going somewhere you're not, not anytime soon, so we might as well get rid of the drug addicts and derelicts,* she says as the kids work diligently, decorating cakes with rocks, sticks and weeds. Dogs bark, horns honk, tires screech, sirens and music blare from all directions. Patti lifts her arm and sprays water on the skin that hangs down sloppily like the future you don't want to believe is coming, the future you never dreamed would be yours.

Where We're At

A car comes barreling down our one-way street, barely missing Terry's kids, so he yells, *Slow down, bro.* The car brakes then reverses to where Terry stands.

What? the passenger yells.

I said slow down, bro; you almost hit my kids, Terry says.

The driver responds, *I ain't your bro,* as smoke billows out of the windows.

There are kids on this street, bro, Terry raises his voice.

You white bitch, I'll get out and kick the bro out yo Pillsbury dough ass.

Terry stands his ground and says, *I'm right here, bro,* as the passenger leans out of the window and surveys the area.

The lady across the street who rents the upstairs apartment yells, *Just slow down, asshole; there are kids here,* from her window. Then Bill and two other guys come off their porch and Patti comes outside in her tattered bathrobe because God forbid she misses anything.

Bring it, Terry says, staring into the car

and the passenger says, *You just gonna call the cops or I would.*

With his kids watching, Terry says, *I am right here, bro.* And I am glad my daughter's at my mom's house because I don't want her to see two men posturing.

Then Mary comes out and strolls over to the car, *Terrance, honey, is that you? How's your grandma? I haven't seen her in years. She still making those blackberry pies?*

The driver puts out his blunt and says, *Alright Ms. Mary, she's doing alright. She still makes those pies, best pies ever. Still sells them at the church.*

Mary moves closer. N*ow, Terrence, you tell her, I am going to stop by soon to see about one of those pies. You tell her that, alright. Now you get on out of here now, you don't need no more trouble, son, and slow down, honey, what's the rush?*

The driver nods, and waves to Mary as the passenger spits out of his window and says, R*emember, bro, we know where you at.*

Mary stands there with her hands on her hips and waits until the car reaches the corner, turns left onto Broadway and disappears.

The Coming, the Going

Cars pull up in front of Bill's house
throughout the night
into the early morning hours,
blaring music and honking horns.
Neighbors peek out through blinds
or turn on their porch lights.
Patti keeps a record of license plate numbers
on a pad she leaves on her nightstand,
even though Henry tells her
to mind her own business.
Sometimes Henry walks out into the night
and comes back hours later
with a cup of gas station coffee.
I could have put on a pot for you, Patti offers
when he returns, even though she knows
he doesn't go out for the coffee.

The Morning Buzz

Before it gets too hot,
I weed our front flower beds
while my daughter draws
a night sky on a shattered sidewalk.
Bill sneaks up on us
and asks my daughter what she is drawing.
She doesn't respond, she's too busy
turning the universe upside down.
I can smell the beer on his breath
from three feet away
He holds a bag of fast food,
dips his hand in and pulls out
a handful of greasy fries
that he shoves into his mouth.
Sad, he says while chewing,
how there are less flower gardens around,
guess people don't want to make the time
to maintain them, he says.
I think about telling him how
the traffic at his house
is getting really annoying,
but he drifts away. I keep pulling,
my daughter keeps drawing,
and the sun beats down unbiasedly
even on the places where
the flowers used to be.

Life on the Outside

Just before going back inside,
I spot Tony, the manager of Burger King,
strolling down the street,
in his work uniform,
with a voluptuous young woman.
He doesn't notice me,
kneeling beside my flower bed.
He is busy talking and laughing.
Today, he is wearing his uniform;
it is not wearing him.
Even his visor finally gets to serve
its intended purpose,
warding off the sun, not grease,
so he can appreciate
the golden beauty
sizzling beside him
like golden french fries
just pulled from the fryer.

Coming Back from War

Even though one of the men living
in the halfway house,
towards the end of our street,
did not come back from Afghanistan,
someone resembling him marches
to the gas station every morning
at 6am sharp to buy the newspaper.

The ruddy-faced man, who shares
a room with him, once confided,
The guy doesn't read a damn word.
he spreads pages all over the floor, cuts
out pictures of people and glues them
on poster boards that he piles under his bed.

Today in the sweltering heat, while
watching the kids toss water balloons
back and forth, the man who did not
come back from Afghanistan,
barrels by us like a tank.
He's cloaked in a heavy camouflaged jacket.

Patti, the neighborhood busybody scowls,
Why is he allowed to walk around here like that?
And I just stand there watching as my daughter
cups her hands and waits patiently for
her friend to toss her a water balloon.
I think of how my father told me
that when he came back from Vietnam,
he saw protestors spit on soldiers.

The red balloon travels through the air,
lands in my daughter's hands,
bounces out, hits the ground
and bursts, just like the words
I want to speak to Patti, but don't.

A Handful of Rocks

While I scrape old paint from our front steps in preparation for a fresh coat, Terry drives up, slams his truck door, and curses about how a teenager, a block over, just threw a handful of rock at his windshield. He holds a piece of ripped cloth in his hand, and yells, *I almost had that little punk, almost had him.* I study the lightening storm of cracks on his windshield. My daughter sweeps paint chips from the steps into a plastic pail. *I don't have glass insurance! It's always something,* he yells. I nod, thinking about all the things we don't have money to replace. He stomps inside his house, clenching a piece of the culprit's shirt. I hear him telling the story to Chrissy in greater detail.

I keep scrapping and my daughter keeps sweeping old chips into her red pail. I have been thinking about how living things survive or thrive under certain conditions, how the flowers I planted in the front yard don't get enough sun, how I should transplant the ferns in the backyard up here and move these flowers someplace else, how if we weren't just scrapping by like everyone else here, I would move into the woods to distance myself from the handful of rocks life throws at us.

What Was Once Ours

Mary's lived in this neighborhood
for decades, raised four sons
and now her granddaughter here.
Two of her sons have spent more time
in prison than out,
one died of an overdose,
the other spends more time
working than living
and still barely makes ends meet.
Her husband died too young
and left her with debt.
Even with all this, she goes on
smiling more than frowning.
Today, she is outside spray painting
her garbage cans fluorescent pink.
When I ask, she says that last night
was the third time this year
that her trash can disappeared.
Who would take someone's trash cans?
she asks as she waves away the paint fumes,
I mean really, who does that?
I nod and think about property
that has gone missing:
Chrissy's American flag,
the Finelli's garden gnomes,
and Patti's welcome mat.
I consider why people take from others
who are struggling just like them
as Mary destroys her own property
just to keep it from being seized.

How to Trick Bats

We toss pebbles up into the sky,
watch bats swoop down;
this is my daughter's first lesson in dishonesty,

repeat, repeat, repeat.

Braids

Nina's sitting on her front porch stairs
watching the kids ride their bicycles.
My daughter and Chrissy's daughter
ride over and ask her what she's doing.
Watching you, Nina says.
Us? my daughter asks.
Yea you, you girls are so lucky
and you don't even know it, she says.
The girls throw their bikes down
on the grass and sit beside Nina.
They smile and giggle.
I hear my daughter say,
No, I chase boys, and Nina advises,
Let them chase you.
Terry moves close to me and whispers,
Did you hear about her dad?
He's looking at 15 years for dealing, 15 years.
I look over and Nina's playing with
my daughter's hair
and I think how she'll be our age
when her father gets out.
I don't know how she does it,
her nimble fingers
weave my daughter's short, thin
hair into two flawless braids.

Fireworks during a Recession

While fireworks explode over the river,
I admire the muted crackling and popping
on my daughter's and husband's faces,
involuntary muscles kick in when the mind
travels outside the body
to witness a speculator event.
Last night's argument over spending more
than we have seems insignificant.

There is no exchange rate in the currency
of this moment, just our daughter's hands
reaching up into the night sky
to pick a sizzling bouquet,
and my husband's runaway tears
watering the flowers before they disappear.
After smoke disperses
there will be no evidence
of this burst of emotion,
just a crowd of people fighting
their way back to their cars,
their lives,
their troubles.

The Zipper

While rotating and spinning in midair,
he asks, *Did you hear that?*
then adds, *stripped bolt bearings.*
This is the moment a poet regrets
marrying a machinist.
My eyes have been
clenched since I said *yes*
and my stomach turned as soon
as the operator checked our door.

A few weeks, after leaving for
graduate school, across the country,
I called to say I was pregnant.
He said he'd come up
with the cash to fly to San Francisco,
hung up the phone, took his savings,
all two hundred dollars, drove
to the closest casino, and sat
at the first blackjack table he saw.

Now suspended at the top,
swaying as occupants slowly unload,
my husband shifts his weight
to flip my nerves.
When he came back
broke from the casino,
my period had arrived tsunami style.
He cackles now, knowing
the feeling of being turned
upside down,
nauseated by movement
without gaining any ground.

Fishing

Chrissy and I sit on her porch steps, discussing
where we'd vacation if we could afford to,
while our kids cast jump ropes, makeshift fishing rods,
from the porch into overgrown grass.
Terry comes out and announces, *Henry is having an affair*
with that redhead attendant who works the overnight
at the corner gas station, you know the one who double bags
everything you get, even if it is just a single pack of gum.
Neither I nor any fish will bite, but that doesn't stop our kids
from trying to attach live earthworms onto imaginary hooks,
or Terry from expounding on Henry's indiscretions.
Now suddenly I regret never going fishing with my father
as a kid, only watching the aftermath, how he held the fish
firmly as he scraped from tail to head with the back of a knife
to remove the scales, how they would adhere to him,
travel with him like the past, clinging desperately.

Self-Portrait of Fish Scales and Diamonds

My father scraped the scales from fish,
starting just above the tail,
with the back of a heavy knife
while sharing words of wisdom:
Cold-running water loosens the scales.
Take your time or the scales will fly all over.
A man loves a woman who can clean fish.
I listened as I placed a shiny scale
above the knuckle of my ring finger.

Thirty years later, a marquise diamond
rests where fish scales once did,
and I have yet to clean a fish.
Since my husband can't stand the smell,
I only cook them when
we're arguing. As he frantically opens
windows, I look down at my ring
and recite the steps my father taught me
as if it were my mantra.

Welcome Mat

First the banging, then: *Mama, Mama! MAMA!*
I draw back curtains
and see one of Mary's sons, standing at her door.
Come on Mama, just let me in!
Neighbors peek out to witness him
banging with one hand
and holding a bouquet of flowers in the other.
Mama, please, Mama, I just need, he shouts
falling to his knees on the welcome mat,
resting his head against the door.
Then the sirens, the flashing lights.
He jumps up, drops the flowers,
leaps over the side of the porch,
bolts into the backyard
where he'll climb the chain link fence to freedom.
A few minutes later,
the cop meanders to Mary's door,
taking inventory of his surroundings,
then stands on the offering her son left.
Mary opens the door, but doesn't come out.
When the cop leaves, we all go back
to what we were doing,
but I can't stop wondering about those flowers
abandoned on Mary's welcome mat,
if any of the other nosy neighbors noticed
the bulbs still dangling from the stems.

Parades

Joe, who lives to the left of us,
is outside with the other guys
who live with him, trying to
start a beat-up, old pickup truck.
Joe owns his house, but rents out rooms
to his construction crew,
so he can save up enough money
to marry his on-again, off-again
girlfriend Sue.
When Joe gets the truck started,
they all cheer and pat each other
on the back like they just won
a basketball game.
I owe you man, one of the guys says
and Joe just smiles.
Joe's family has had a tough year.
Once pillars, now pariahs,
of the community,
after Joe's brother killed
a young mother and her child
in a DWI accident.
*I'm glad my father isn't around
to see this,* Joe told my husband.
His father, once the city's fire chief,
dressed up in a dalmatian costume
for thirty-three years worth of parades
to toss candy from the fire truck to the city kids.

The End of the Summer

Terry is outside, driving his remote control car
down the street, while his kids cheer.
Chrissy hasn't slept yet, she just got back
from her overnight baking gig and is pissed;
the sink is full of dirty dishes,
everything taken out wasn't put away,
and her husband is entertaining their kids
by crashing his man toy into the neighbors' trash cans.
She comes out on the porch and yells,
Why don't you take those Christmas lights down?
Terry laughs, *Why would I do that now?*
I'll just have to put them back up in a few months.

Section 2: Stop

Stop

While waiting to pick up my daughter at her bus stop,
besides the normal cursing and complaints,
I overhear one of the mothers bragging
about how her husband got out of a traffic ticket.
Apparently, he cut some branches down
from trees in his backyard,
brought them to the sign,
he was accused of running,
and had her hold the branches up
to create a visual obstruction,
so he could take a photo to bring to court.

The Party

After Bill, the neighbor
on the other side of Terry's house,
throws a horseshoe through
Terry's garage window,
Terry goes over screaming,
but within a half hour,
he's showing the other men up,
throwing five ringers in a row.

Later Terry's wife, Chrissy,
brings over maple bacon cupcakes
just pulled from the oven,
and everyone's happy,
even Bill, who's manipulating
cardboard from an empty beer case
to duct tape over his mistake.

Once Patti told me
Bill was married to a Ukrainian woman,
who had a glass eye and
the only thing I could think to ask was
Could she still blink?

How to Write a Letter You Don't Want Anyone to Read

Dear Andy Rooney,

Like our cat, you died last night from surgical complications.
I've learned that what should be routine is always anything but.

I want you to know I cannot carry our cat's stiff body past
her two kittens and my daughter into the backyard
where I dug a hole to bury her, so she is lying in her kitty litter.

I feel guilty, Andy, I really, really do. I've learned that using
the adverb "really" is unnecessary, but I can't help myself.

Truth be told, I watched you because *60 Minutes* often runs late
and is on before our favorite show. I always told you to talk

faster, but you never listened and my husband muttered about
how if you could make money writing then anyone could,

but to be honest, Andy, every once in awhile you made him
chuckle, which in turn made me jealous. My words don't do that

for him, so I do what I always do: leave with our daughter, leave
my husband's dinner wrapped in tin foil, still warm on the stove,

leave a detailed note explaining why I couldn't bury our cat and
leave the shovel sticking up in a pile of dirt beside the hole.

How to Make a Leaf Rubbing

While we search our yard for leaves,
Chrissy opens her kitchen window
and calls me over. She has been
at Dubbon's Bakery for months,

but doesn't like it. *There's a guy there*
more interested in kneading me than
the dough, she confesses, *Terry would kill*
if he knew, but we really need this job.

As my daughter collects leaves in
a brown paper bag, I recall jobs I've had
where this behavior was the norm,
how I've been trapped like easy prey

in my share of walk-ins, arms overflowing
with condiments, hoping to talk
my way out. Later my daughter will
place a sheet of paper over the leaves,

rub gently with crayons until
an imprint appears. I think about
how I want something different
for her, not a reproduction of this life.

Dancing Under the Streetlights

A man's voice screams:
You said you'd meet me
at Burger King! Where you at, bitch?
I look through the blinds and catch
Patti peeking out through her blinds.
Dogs bark. Porch lights turn on.
You better get the fuck down here!
A man paces back and
forth in the middle of the street.
He is talking into a phone.
He is on an asphalt stage.
Bitch, don't hang up on me,
I will reach through this phone
and slap you silly.
It is closer to 1am than midnight.
Sirens sound in the distance.
An approaching car's headlights
shine on the man, but he does not budge.
More porch lights turn on.
The driver honks
and the man says, *What, what?*
you want some of this?
The driver honks again, but the man
does not move, he just stands there,
yelling into the phone.
When the car tries to go around him,
he steps back into the car's path,
so the car tries to go around the other way
and just like that, back and forth,
under the street lights,
the yelling man and honking car
dance.

The Turn

While watching my daughter ride her bicycle
with the other kids, Terry tells me how Henry
sold his brother a lemon. *The car's clutch cable
went and it costs more than it is worth to fix.
Freaking used car salesmen!*
He goes on about how the end of the paving season
is nearing and how it is going to be a tough winter.
*You wouldn't know anything about that being
a teacher and all, you get paid all year long,
and it's not like you can get fired,* he adds.
I admire how the wind lifts my daughter's hair
as she races around, how her smile is the result
of joy rather than sarcasm or vengeance.
When does it happen? When exactly do we turn
on one another, like the female Praying Mantis
who, after satisfying her needs, devours her mate?

Morning Toast

Bill and one of his housemates
lean over the railing of his front porch,
drinking beers and taking in the day.
Bill offers the kids a few boxes of bang snaps.
As the kids toss them onto pavement
to detonate them, Bill asks Terry,
Did you hear about how the guy
who bought the candy apple lady's house
is fixing it up and renting it to
the Mexicans for 1600 a month?
When I say that is pretty high,
Bill's housemate says, *Not for 20 people,*
and they laugh. He raises his beer,
smashes it into Bill's
and says, *To the neighborhood!*

I Got It This Time

Outside on her porch,
Chrissy confesses that
their children qualified
for reduced lunch this year,
but she is ashamed of this—
she whispers,
and looks around
to make sure no one heard.
A reduced lunch tastes
the same as a regular lunch
to an empty stomach, I say
and wish I could give more
to her than verbal reassurances.
Later the ice cream truck
comes around and I see her
cringe, the way I often do
when reminded of what
I can't afford, but
am forced to buy anyway.
Isn't it late in the season?
I mean, it is closer to winter
than summer,
Chrissy asks as our kids,
who are wearing sweatshirts,
flag down the truck.
Guess everyone is looking
to make a little extra cash,
I laugh. She is saying no
to her kids, but I say,
I got it this time, as I pull
a ten dollar bill from my pocket
and think about how lucky
we are to have one another.

Because Ice Cream Always Melts

Terry walks outside to find the kids
eating ice cream and he gives
Chrissy that look like "you know
we can't spend our money frivolously"
and I say, *Oh, I paid, I owed Chrissy.*
I am kind of telling the truth
because I kind of do, for all the times
she has done for me and Terry looks
relieved because every penny matters.
He sits down and watches the ice cream
melting down our kids arms,
how carefree they are, unaware of what goes on
behind the scenes, how everything costs.
Everything. And Terry is thinking
on the same plane as I am and says,
They will understand way too soon.
Then Chrissy adds, *Don't you wish someone
would invent ice cream that never melted?*
And we all nod.

If Ice Cream Never Melted

Joe's outside unloading boxes
from his truck and my husband
goes over, picks up a box
and starts helping.
Joe tells him how Sue is moving in
because she hurt herself and is out of work.
He's happy because he loves her
and she needs him for now.
My husband asks how his brother's doing
and he responds, *His birthday was yesterday*
and my mom went to see him,
says he made a birthday cake out of
two packs of cookies, a tube of peanut butter
and three bags of M&Ms
that he bought from the commissary
and shared with his cellmates.
He called it correctional cake, no joke,
correctional cake, Joe shakes his head,
My mom came home and cried all day,
took a gallon of rocky road ice cream
out of the freezer because it was his favorite
and let it melt on her kitchen counter.
Then, leaning against the tailgate,
Joe asks, *How could something like this*
ever happen to us?

How to Find Your Way Back Home

A third house on our block went into foreclosure.
The cats, left behind, spray our backdoor,
use our daughter's sandbox as an outhouse,
and now, on Halloween evening, they weave
in and out of trick-or-treaters and shadows,
looking for a familiar face to bring them home.

We dress our daughter like a princess,
walk half-a-dozen blocks away from our home,
up a steep hill to where the fancy houses are.
There are no welcome mats here, just a sliver
of moonlight revealing the stillness
of well-manicured lives, the gentle glow
of televisions flickering like flames escaping
through the faces of jack-o-lanterns.
We ring a dozen doorbells before realizing
these people aren't going to answer their doors.

Our daughter, noticing our disappointment,
tells us not to worry. She holds her glow stick
upright like her convictions and tells us
she will lead us back home. I can't
help considering all the extravagances
she may never know as we venture back
to our one-way street, pass by the woman
who pushes a plastic baby doll around
in a stroller, crack heads, ghosts, psychiatric
patients, prostitutes, witches, vampires,
zombies, princesses, punk rockers and hungry cats
who circle around us like debt collectors.

When we round the corner of our street,
our lunatic neighbor, Crazy Kay, is teetering
on the road's yellow dividing line, greeting people
as if she's standing at her own front door.
Kay's in her seventies and dressed in an authentic-

looking Native American Chief costume.
When the Chief holds out a five gallon
paint bucket filled with loose candy corn and says,
Welcome, pilgrim, some call this holiday
Halloween, but I like to call it Thanks Giving,
I know we have found our way back home.

How to Tell the Truth

After our daughter falls asleep wearing her Halloween costume,
her fingers still laced around a glow-in-the-dark wand,
candy wrappers crumbled around her like a sky littered
with exhausted dreams, we go out onto the porch to discuss
how to pay bills. I mention how we'll inevitably bounce checks
while you smoke a cigarette. Maybe, I yell about how I'm tired
of juggling debt from credit card to credit card and I'm not sure if
it is really a cigarette that you are smoking.

You may have told me to stop being a bitch, but you would never
say that, would you? With a mouthful of tootsie rolls, I threaten
to leave, but there's only a half tank of gas in my car and without
your doctorate degree in jerry-rigging, the car won't get me far.

I don't have faith in much anymore, just a sliver of moonlight revealing
the stillness of your convictions. Before I finish complaining,
you walk away, just like that, without saying anything or maybe
I walk away and go inside to wash the dishes because you're not
giving me the answers I want. I stand at the sink and let the water run
like thoughts rushing down pipes, away from me. You go upstairs
to bed, and I am annoyed you can fall asleep so quickly.
What gives you the right, to close your eyes and just let go like that?

How to Paint in the Dark

After the hurricane took away our electricity
we open the curtains, sit at the kitchen table,
pull out acrylic paint, brushes and canvas.

There are crickets chirping and it is daytime.
I overhear the neighbors to the right of us
discussing the possibility of meat going bad,

pounds and pounds of venison and pork chops.
They will grill it all and invite family over.
Our neighbor, to the left, talks about losing

a bid for a job; this is the third consecutive time;
he just can't charge any less. He has to pay for
insurance. Now this, the high winds blowing off

shingles, flood waters engulfing cars, seeping
through foundations, collecting and sitting
stagnant, growing foul. Our neighbor behind us

is beating his dog because his wife left him.
My daughter looks out windows; she wants
to see thunder. As soon as I tell her that you can

only hear it, she looks defeated. I wonder why
humans steal each others' faith. The dog cowers
in the bushes that separate our yards and I know

even if our phone worked, I wouldn't call the police.

Potholes

Terry's outside trimming
the hedges between our houses
when Crazy Kay comes by
and trips in the road
in front of his house.
Damn potholes, she yells
as Terry comes over
and extends his hand.
The only way to get anything done
around here is to threaten to sue,
just leave me right here
and call an ambulance, she says.
But before he can dial the number,
she is standing up, chuckling and
wiping the dirt off. *Just kidding,*
she says, then goes on, *You know*
once I fell over on West Chestnut
on some guy's sidewalk and
said the same thing, well
I let that hunka-hunka burning love
carry me all the way home,
I just wanted to see what
I could get out of you, she winks.

How I Learned to Make the Best Pecan Pie, Ever

Sue, Joe's girlfriend, just moved in.
She was waiting tables at the diner
right off the thruway
until she broke her ankle.
Today, while raking wet leaves
in our backyard, I watch her
move boxes of their stuff
out to their shed to make room for herself.
Balancing on one crutch, she pushes,
tosses, then kicks the boxes.
When I overhear her cry out
in pain, I go to the fence,
dividing our lives,
and ask if she's alright.
She hobbles over and confesses,
I want to go back to work,
I miss my regulars.
They're much less demanding
than these hooligans, plus
it's too much dealing with
Joe's family tragedy,
she laughs.
We both lean against the fence
as if it will support the weight
of our worries.
I ask why she's wearing
a waitress apron
if she's not working
and she pulls out all types of things:
a cell phone, a house phone,
the TV remote, scissors, rubber bands,
proving the apron's usefulness.
We talk about men, waiting tables,
unexpected tragedies and domestication.
She pulls out a pad from her apron
and writes down a family recipe
for the best pecan pie ever
then passes it to me
over the rusty metal fence.

The Magic Show

When he makes water disappear before our eyes,
my daughter becomes an immediate convert
while I grapple with basic principles of physics,
introduced to me as a stoned high school senior.

Why, as we get older, do we try to disprove the
existence of magic, question explanations not
readily available to the eye? Can the dollar bill
the magician takes from a woman in the front row

and the love that my husband and I search
every nook and cranny of our house for
really vanish, just like that? When did love change
from a concept to a commodity? My daughter asks,

Can you teach me how to make things disappear?
Even though I know matter cannot be created or
destroyed, I nod. I don't have a top hat or a rabbit,
but I have been doing just that for years and then

the tears come. In response, she uses her sleeve
to wipe my face. *You're already learning,* I tell her,
but I am not sure what kind of magic will help
her understand how to conserve what really matters.

conservation of matter: a fundamental principle of classical physics that
matter cannot be created or destroyed

How to Survive without Plumbing

While you solder pipes in the basement
I think about how before plumbing
people held their water cups steady,
how each decision had an immediate consequence,
how families stayed together and close to water.

And now our daughter needs to go potty
to feed her addiction to flushing until her hands
are guided away. It is going to be hours you said
before you started, so if you have to go,

go now—which reminds me of the start of
long car trips with my father, how he never stopped,
fixed on a destination invisible to adolescent eyes.
The burning of metal being joined together

wafts up the stairs where I sip thick coffee,
microwaved several times, sit cross-legged
thinking about what I want versus what will be
like water, directed through pipes, left option-less.

Recession Tooth Fairy

The third tooth lost
in one weekend,
another dangles.
I pray my daughter won't
lose another until
I get paid
next week.
We have already
scavenged under
couch cushions.

Garbage Night

As I bring out my garbage cans,
I overhear Nina screaming
You don't get it! as she pounces
off the porch and heads toward Broadway.
Mary stands on the porch for a minute
then turns around and goes inside—
All our intentions are colorful balloons
that slip from our fingers and drift away.

How to Stop the Snoring

Right now, as you snore into your pillow,
rescue workers and volunteers comb

through the wreckage for survivors.
When I wake you up to let you know

I can't handle your snoring, you say
you feel the same way about mine. But I was
not sleeping and I don't even snore, do I?

Like a tornado, you tell me and I laugh
at the idea of being compared to a force

of nature that has catastrophic consequences.
Later when you fall back to sleep, I nudge you

until you turn over, breathe freely for a little while.
There is someone asleep right now in a house

that will be in ruins by sunrise. They may or
may not be snoring. This is what the world is

about—the whirring and roaring of moments,
fighting to find that same comfortable position

night after night, nature taking its revenge
the only way it knows how, while we are asleep.

How to Avoid a War

Our daughter pedals then brakes,
asks you to push her again, pedals
then breaks. She is learning how
to trust a world that moves rapidly
below her rotating feet. You

worry about elbow and knee pads,
all the safety measures we fail
to provide. I am preoccupied with
politics, run ahead to point out
pending ruts. A boy, riding a bicycle

in the opposite direction, darts toward
us; his mother trails behind screaming,
Slow down. As she passes she covers
her eyes and says she's not cut out for
this job. I yell, *this is exactly how the*

presidential candidates see the looming
war in Iran, and you give me that look
and shake your head. You don't want me
to explain this abstract metaphor, but know
I will try. It is like how we each negotiate

with fate, as if we are more worried about
how we will be perceived if we are wrong,
rather than doing what is right. If there is a
right. You say that I don't make sense.
Our daughter stops short, jumps off her bicycle,

grabs the bag of stale rolls from her basket.
She is ready to feed the ducks in the river,
that is beside the path. The bicycle pedals
are still in motion; so is your head that
sways back and forth like a bone-white flag.

To the Kids Who Tried to Steal Our Bikes

When I pull into the driveway,
Patti comes over and as soon as
I open my car door, she lectures:
You really shouldn't leave
your bikes out; I had to chase
some kids out of your yard today.
I thank her as I try to unload groceries.
Bags hang from my arms while
Patti goes on a tirade about today's youth.
The ice cream I bought is melting
and to be honest I wish they took
the bikes, it would free up some room
for us to collect new futile dreams.

How to Catch a Fish

By the creek, we watch a couple fishing off the dock.
They stand about eight feet apart, so passersby
wouldn't think they're together, but we stick around
to watch them pull up catfish. They untangle hooks from
whiskery faces then throw them back. They're a contemporary
variant of *The Old Man and the Sea*, struggle, defeat and death.

The woman throws her pole down and runs over to him
every time his line tightens. *Here, let me help,* she offers.
Woman, go back there, you scaring my fish on purpose,
he says, shooing her away. Like a deflating balloon, she lets out
a full-belly laugh that spreads like a ripple in water.

See what I put up with, the man says, looking at my husband,
who nods and looks away from me. *You an old man, you can use*
all the help you can get, the woman counters, leaning over the dock.
He pulls and his line flies up. *Woman, now look what you done did,*
that fish done took my bait, he says, slapping her rear end.
No, I took the bait and pulled up a cranky, old catfish, she says, winking at me.

I'd do anything for this kind of love, pure and simple just before dusk.

How to Put a Fish to Bed

"Fish," he said softly, aloud, "I'll stay with you until I am dead."
—Ernest Hemingway

I have been reading *The Old Man and The Sea*
to my four-year-old daughter until she falls asleep,
averaging three to four pages each night.
For weeks now, we've been in the skiff
with Santiago struggling with the marlin,
holding the line for him when he gets too weary.
Each night, her last words dangle helplessly in the air
like everything else we haven't gotten around to yet:
When are we going to catch the fish?

During our days, my husband and I struggle
to keep our cars running, our bills paid,
and food on the table. I have been questioning if
there really is honor in struggle, defeat, then death,
until tonight when finally he harpoons the marlin
through the heart. I look over at her and she asks
What we are we going to do now? but before I have a
worthy answer, a cloud of blood disperses into

shark infested waters and she drifts toward dreams.

On Marriage

After a full day's work,
he works,
the way my father did.

After boards drop
on his foot,
possibly breaking a bone
or two,
he eats dinner,
brings his plate
to the sink
then limps back out
to work,
because *things need to get done.*

When he comes back in,
he tightens
a doorknob,
replaces the refrigerator light,
then tinkers with
one of our daughter's broken toys.

After he falls asleep
in dusty jeans,
I take a screwdriver
out of his pocket,
and slowly remove
his boots one at a time;
this is what
I do.

How to Resolve a Case of Mistaken Identity

This is not the first time something of this nature
has happened. At a supermarket in San Francisco,
ten years ago, I heard a woman screaming, *Marilyn,*
Marilyn, before tapping me on the shoulder. *Marilyn,*
it has been years, how are you? she asked, hugging me
when I turned around. I stepped back, looked down
at the conveyor belt moving my box of noodles
and two cans of diced tomatoes toward the cashier.

Today an Income Execution letter came in the mail
addressed to me from the local sheriff's office.
The maiden name and social security number aren't
an exact match. Frantically, I call to remedy
this mysterious debt crisis, before my employer
is contacted and my wages garnished.
A clerk at the sheriff's office, in a disbelieving tone,
tells me that there is a process involved in proving
who I am and explains the steps I need to take.

The day I became Marilyn, the cashier said the total
was two dollars and eighty-three cents and I said
Great, great, it has been a long time, hasn't it?
to the woman who mistook me as an old friend.
As I handed over three dollars, it dawned on me
that for a little while I didn't have to be a broke,
graduate student, who just walked nine blocks
because I didn't have enough money for groceries
and public transportation; I didn't have to be a lonely
New Yorker working as a dishwasher at the
college's cafeteria, so I could afford to study poetry.
Yes, poetry. I didn't have to miss my lover who was
2, 911 miles away. I could be Marilyn,

Marilyn, who married a surgeon. Marilyn, who
traveled the world and doesn't need to work.
Marilyn, who let an old friend sum up the last ten years
of her life then embraced her for a second time
before parting. Marilyn, who took a strange woman's
phone number and promised to keep in touch.

When Things Break

On what was supposed to be
their last job of the season,
one of Terry's brothers overturns the roller.
Now they are in Terry's driveway
trying to get it running again,
so they can finish paving tomorrow.
When my husband gets home,
Terry calls him over to look at the wiring
and within a few minutes
the men are cheering.
Later during dinner,
my husband tells me that work
is slowing down again,
that men are breaking things
just so they have something to fix.

A Lobster's Home

On Thanksgiving, everyone brings.
My uncle boils the lobsters
we will eat in lieu of turkey,
claws instead of wings.
The women put out
crackers and picks,
troughs of melted butter
and empty bowls for shells.
Even though most of us moved
off the Island, everything and every-
one we love comes from water.
My brother worked on a lobster boat
with other men in our family
when he was still in high school.
Now he is losing his house,
deciding whether to
make the bank take it from him
or simply give it back.
I pick every last crevice,
even suck the meat from the
antennas and eat the red eggs
hiding at the end of my
husband's tail as he and my
daughter look on in disgust.
It's alright, really, I try to
convince them in the same tone
my brother used when he told me
he stopped paying his mortgage.

At the Corner of How and Why

In the morning's newspaper,
an article about how
Joe's brother's trial
is being postponed again,
this time until after the holidays.
The victims' family is quoted
as saying that their wounds
will never heal.
Last week, Joe lost a bid
on a job that he thought
was guaranteed,
the week before he lost two.
Even during the recession,
Joe told my husband,
this didn't happen.

This afternoon, I ran into
Sue at the corner,
leaning against her crutches,
waiting for the bus.
She told me that this morning
while Joe's mother
was getting a root canal,
her dentist asked her
how her son was enjoying jail
when she couldn't answer
because his hands were in her mouth,
he continued, *Well, he will get*
what he deserves where he is going.
Then he pulled and pried and drilled
while Joe's mother squirmed
in the chair for another forty-five minutes.

Section 3: Dead End

_____

Dead End

After her neighbors reported her
to the health department for animal hoarding,
Crazy Kay made a series of signs that she posted
in her yard facing their house including:
"GO BACK TO NEW JERSEY!"
"KEEP OUT JOISY!!"
"MY DOGS WON'T BITE YOU, BUT I WILL!"
Apparently she called the building department
on them for putting an illegal addition on their house
and is suing them for defamation of character.
Terry jokes, *Maybe the Dead End sign*
should be changed to: Beware Combat Zone.

The American Dream

Mr. Finelli works all day
wrapping Christmas lights
around the railing and spindles
on this porch.
He hangs them from the roof,
doorways and windowsills;
when he is all done
and plugs in the lights—

darkness.

Where Once There Were Candy Apples

While scraping frost from my car windows,
I notice the smell of skunk wafting through the air,
and then hear Terry, who's warming up his vehicle, too.
He comes up behind me and asks, *You smell that?*
Yeah, smells like a family of skunk got taken out, I shiver.
Nah, Terry says, *It's coming from that house*
with the boarded-up windows,
the one the old lady and her daughter used to live in,
the one some dude bought for fifty thousand cash.
I bet he is using it as a grow house.
I tug at the edges of my gloves, trying to cover bare skin.

Before the old lady and her daughter died,
the only time we would really talk to them
was on Halloween,
when they'd hand out homemade candy apples,
so magnificent that the whole neighborhood
would sit for awhile on their rotting wicker chairs
and creaky old porch, trying to figure out the best way
to bite into their shiny gifts.

Shoveling out from Under

As we shovel out from under
this year's first storm,
I overhear Terry
tell Henry
about how his transmission
just went.
Henry counters:
Yeah, our dryer is dying,
even after three hours
my jeans are still damp.
Feel them, he urges,
they are seriously frozen.

I laugh to myself
because today
we are the lucky ones;
our refrigerator's compressor motor
stopped working this morning,
but we put the contents
in a hallowed-out snowdrift
until my husband has time
to tinker with the wires.

Snow Angels

We walk in new snow.
There is only one other set of footprints,
so my daughter and I follow them
to the end of our road
where Crazy Kay is clearing her sidewalk.
As she turns to us, she falls,
disappearing behind a mound of snow,
so we run to where she is and
find her on the ground, flailing her arms and legs.

I wonder if this is what a heart attack looks like
and wish I paid more attention
in high school health class
when my teacher taught us how to revive CPR Annie,
counting and pushing on her plastic chest.

Instead, I focused on the hot skate boarder
who spent the class touching
the razor-sharp tips of his bleached blonde mohawk
with the palm of his hand.
God, I was in love then, so in love that I studied
the writing on his torn jeans
as if punk rock bands and the anarchy symbol
would be covered on the final.

Then my daughter drops to the ground too,
right beside Crazy Kay,
mimicking her movements.
Initially mortified that she is impersonating
a dying woman, I yell at her to get up,
then realize what they are doing.

I wonder where that skateboarder is now,
after all these years as I watch
my daughter and Crazy Kay fan their limbs.
Does he remember CPR or like me

just the story our teacher told about how
Annie's face was modeled after the death mask,
a plaster cast of an unidentified woman,
who committed suicide by jumping
into the Seine River in Paris, France.

The Black Angel

Mary got a new job
at the midtown laundromat,
four days a week,
for horrible pay,
no health benefits or retirement,
just endless loads of
free laundry.
She confesses she stopped by
the nursing home, crept into
the client's room,
who accused her of stealing,
and placed a black angel figurine
amongst the other religious chachkas
on the woman's dresser.
When I ask her why she says,
You must not be Catholic.
I explain how I am one generation removed.
Well, honey, she says, *A real Catholic*
wouldn't dare get rid of an angel,
no matter if it were cracked, wingless or black.
And that woman, Mrs. Harris, who accused me
of stealing, because she didn't want a black aide,
will have to hold onto that angel
like the truth until the day she dies,
and child, that makes
starching strangers' shirts a little less painful.

Popcorn Proposal

While grabbing the mail, I see Sue hobbling on one crutch, trying to carry groceries. When I go over to help, she says, *I can't do this anymore.* She hands the bags over to me and collapses to her knees then scoots around onto her backside. Patti's blinds open; I wave, and then Patti disappears. *Joe asked me to marry him,* she explains, *because I'm pregnant.* In lieu of congratulations, I ask about her ankle, which is swollen as if newly injured. I take frozen peas from one of the bags and ask Sue to take off the waitress apron she has been wearing around her waist to stow her necessities. I empty it, put a bag of frozen peas, from her groceries, in the front pocket and fasten it around her ankle. *Wow, genius,* she says. *Tricks of the trade,* I respond, sitting down beside her. She nods. *He took me out to see some stupid action movie and slipped the ring into the popcorn bucket,* she says, showing me her ring, *and all I can think about is the God damn breakfast line cook. Plus, I mean, he has been through so much this year; how can I say no?*

The Best Christmas Card Ever

Taped to our front door,
I find a Christmas card
addressed to us, possibly,
since our last name is butchered,
but the sender's signature is clear:
Crazy Kay, aka Santa Sauce and zoo!
Inside, wishes for
a Merry Christmas
a Happy New Year
and inspired poetry!
Written on top of
a white removable adhesive label
still visible underneath:
Happy Holidays, Kay!
Love, Frank and Helen.

How to Work on Cars

They both hope it's not the carburetor,
the device that blends air and fuel.
My husband and his brother try to
squeeze under the hood at the same time
looking for answers. If you did not know
them, you would never guess they
grew inside the same womb, these two
men standing side by side in the driveway
on Christmas Eve. The horror of having to
take everything out of its chest
weighs heavy on their expressions:
neither of them have bought a single
gift yet, and the sun is already setting.

The Force of Fingers

It's Christmas Day and I am in love with you again,
not because we are religious or anything,
just because before the sun came up,
you made deviled eggs
and meticulously wrapped the gifts
you bought last night from The Salvation Army:
a pair of pink fuzzy boots (two sizes too small) for our daughter,
a toaster (that only tans one side of the bread at a time) for me,
and a remote control car that still doesn't work right
even after replacing the batteries,
but you'll tinker with it until
the tires turn without the force of fingers.

In Time for Dessert

As I unload groceries, Terry pops up behind me and says Patti's husband, Henry,
left on Christmas Eve, but she still had his entire family over, served them
a three course meal and convinced them he got called into work, but that
he would be back in time for dessert, but he never made it. I stand there with
seven plastic bags hanging from my arms like bulky ornaments weighing down
branches as Terry goes on, *I mean, she actually told them he got called into work as if he*
were a doctor, not a used car salesman. When he didn't show, she pretended to call him.
I am sure Henry had dessert alright, the redhead at the gas station.

Saving Ourselves on a Wednesday Afternoon

On our front porch,
I discover
a stack of religious pamphlets,
each one the same.
The distributor must believe
we are in need of serious redemption
or maybe just wanted
to get the job done and go home early.

My daughter counts then tells
me there are twenty-seven.
I open one up, and read:
Nobody else can save you.
Trust in Jesus today!

We fold the pamphlets into airplanes,
throw them into snowbanks
in the backyard; we will collect
the carnage in spring.

Manning the Machines

Since someone has to man
the machines tomorrow,
and that someone is my husband,
we only have one glass
of cheap champagne
and pass out before the ball drops,
only to be awoken by
New Year's fireworks
and Terry screaming,
Oh crap, I think that one landed
on Mark and Becky's roof.

New Years at Soap and Suds

Mary tells me how at first
she was pissed she had to work
at the laundromat on New Year's Eve,
until about eleven thirty when
a man came in with only two items,
stripped down to his boxer shorts,
threw his clothes into the washer
then proceeded to jog
in front of one of the televisions
to keep warm. Mary laughs,
Boy, did I get to see the ball drop!

January

January is frozen between
Christmas and Valentine's day,
suspended like a memory
you want to forget.
Mary and Nina are outside
chipping ice
from the sidewalk in front of Patti's house;
they understand inheriting the duties
of those who abandon you.
Patti watches them from her window
thinking about how Henry
was married when they met,
how she kissed him anyway
and didn't even think
about the other woman.

Warm Cookies

I'm outside, using a broom
to free the icicles from
our gutters when Chrissy comes out
and offers me a plate of
freshly baked oatmeal raisin cookies.
On a frigid afternoon,
in a dismal blue collar neighborhood,
my faith in humanity is restored.

Valentine's Day Tree

Patti's Christmas tree
still looks out
from her front picture window
like a worried wife waiting for
her husband's return.
Over two feet of snow has yet to be
removed from her steps and driveway.
At least Mary and Nina
keep the sidewalk in front clear.
I overhear Chrissy and Terry speculating
on what she is eating;
she hasn't left the house
since Henry split.
Canned food, Terry says.
Grief, Chrissy guesses.
Through the window you can see
that Christmas ornaments
have been replaced
with red, white and pink paper hearts
that hang from the wilting
branches of the last pine tree
that Henry will ever cut down
and bring home to her.

February 15th

On my way to the pharmacy to pick up
reduced priced Valentines and cough medicine,
I see Henry walking toward me with
the redhead gas station attendant.
I climb over a snowbank
and cross the road to avoid awkward conversation.
At the store, a mob of people
with the same idea load their baskets
with 75% off Valentine's goodies,
push and shove to secure mementos of love
turned discount merchandize.
I grab a few items, then leave;
the scene is too much for me
and I can't stop thinking
about how Sue told me she's in love with
the breakfast line cook,
who may actually be the father of her baby.
She told me that the line cook
is married to a woman
who has multiple sclerosis
and can no longer walk to the bathroom alone.
Joe has suffered enough already.
How much can a person take?
On the walk home,
I open up a box of chocolate candies
that contain mystery fillings.
The first one is coconut,
the second caramel,
the third lemon.

Arrests and Avocados

On my way out to get our mail,
Terry catches me and tells me
that yesterday a dozen cop cars
surrounded a house down the block
in the middle of the day.
I thumb through bills
and the grocery circular
as he goes on about how he heard
that another neighbor called CPS
on the family because they
were cooking meth
and beating their children.
As he laments over the downfall
of our community, I am overjoyed
to discover that avocados are on sale
three for a dollar, but I don't tell him this.

Instead, I liken the neighborhood
to a sand mandala, but he thinks
I am referring to the extended happy
hour at the new gay bar that just
opened up on Broadway,
which sets him off on another tirade.
I want to take the time to explain
how the whole neighborhood
is being ritualistically destroyed
to symbolize life's transitory nature,
but these avocados will sell fast,
at least the ripe ones that aren't
scarred by the mass hysteria
of a decent deal out of season.

And the Snow Keeps on Falling

The snow falls faster than
Mary and Nina can shovel.
Why don't you wait until it stops?
Crazy Kay asks as she walks by.
If I waited for things to stop falling
before I picked them up,
I'd be buried alive, Mary answers
and Nina smirks and nods,
agreeing with her grandma
for the first time in years.

Where the Wind Takes the Snow

After spending all day yesterday shoveling,
Mary wakes up to a foot of snow,
a 40 degree house due to
the window Nina uses to sneak out
being left open and puke on her living room carpet.
Even though we didn't shovel yesterday,
the height of the snow in front of our house
is the same height as the snow in front of Mary's
and she is outside cursing the wind
that blew all the bad luck back her way.

The Path Just Shoveled

When the wind dies down,
my husband goes out to shovel.
I dress my daughter
to go out in the snow.
From the window I watch
my husband shoveling a path
and right behind him
my daughter inciting avalanches.

Missing

A little after dinner, Mary comes by
to see if we've seen Nina.
She didn't come home last night
and she didn't go to school today.
I stand in the doorway listening intently
to the fear in Mary's expression,
a hundred different what ifs
distort her face and all I can say is,
She is probably at a friend's house.

How to Pay the Mortgage

Terry snow blows some of the neighbors' sidewalks
and driveways since it is his off-season.
Each time he stops to talk to someone,
he confesses how he can't believe he sold his snowplow
at the end of last winter to pay his mortgage.
I would be rolling in dough if I had held out, he says,
This is the snowiest winter we have had in over a decade.
Everyone is sympathetic; they understand selling out of
desperation, how decisions come back to taunt you
like a Nor'easter late in the season.

Brake-lights

Like with love,
everyone else notices
when one of your brake-lights burns out
before you do.
So as soon as I open
my car door, Patti is on her porch
as if waiting all day right there
to be the bearer of bad news,
Hey, Beck, your right brake light's out,
I noticed it this morning. I hope
you didn't get a ticket, she says,
crossing her arms over her chest,
so her ratty robe covers
her floral moo-moo.
This is the first time I have seen her
since Henry left.
Making up for lost time,
she babbles on
until she's telling me about her cousin Carl,
who went to Mexico a few weeks ago
and ended up hospitalized
for weeks. She screams
from across the street,
You know that thing you get
when you drink dirty water
and you just can't stop crapping,
I mean no matter what you do,
you just keep going and going.

During dinner, when I tell my husband
about the broken light, he nods.
Later from the kitchen window,
I watch him hold a flashlight
between his teeth,
open the trunk of my car,
take off one glove,

unscrew the old bulb,
and exchanges it with a new one.
Just like that and it's fixed—
love is funny that way,
how it can burn out,
how it can be replaced.

The Past Is a Gold Cross Necklace

While driving down Broadway,
I spot Jolene, one of the waitresses
I worked with over a decade ago
at the Dead End Diner,
holding the door
of one of the many pawn shops on Broadway
for Nina, so I pull over.
It has been over a decade since
I have seen Jolene and a week since
Mary has seen Nina.
When I walk into the store,
Jolene turns around, balancing a cardboard box
on her shoulder
as if it is a diner tray.
No way, she says, moving toward me,
I was wondering what happened to you,
she says, *I always figured you would come back*
to the diner again, but you never did.
Nina avoids eye contact;
she stares at the gold cross necklace in her hand.
What you doing here? Jolene asks.
I move closer to Nina, put my hand
on her shoulder and say,
You know just looking for someone special and smile,
Nina's grandmother's been worried sick,
I am gonna give her a ride home now.
Jolene wants to argue, but doesn't,
instead offers, *Yeah, grandmas, they worry.*
That is why I am here, you know, in Kingston.
I am living with my grandmother, taking care of her
in exchange for rent; I was working at the diner,
by the thruway, but it didn't work out.
It's not like the Dead End Diner, she smiles,
I came in to see what I can get for this old stuff,
plus I want to buy my Grandma a sewing machine.
Jolene's skinny, real skinny; I think about asking

her more, but instead say, *Hey, I have a sewing machine*
you can have, here, let me write down my number for you.
Mark bought it for me for Christmas a decade ago
because I wanted to learn to quilt,
but I never got around to learning.
Jolene puts the box down on the counter,
and I can tell she wants to ask me a dozen questions too,
but asking means answering
and we both are itching to get what we came here for.
As I lead Nina out, the man behind the counter yells,
Hey sweetheart, what about that necklace?

Just about Dinner Time

As Nina gets into my car, I grab some books from the seat
and throw them in the back.
You a teacher, right? Nina asks as she settles in.
I am, I answer, then add, *You're grandma has been worried sick.*
She has been going door-to-door asking about you.
Even though it is cold, she opens the car window.
What you teach? she asks.
English and US History.
She changes my radio station. *You like it?*
The music no, teaching yes.
She laughs, puts the cross up in front of her and lets it swing back and forth
like a pendulum.
Why would you get rid of a pretty necklace like that? I ask.
My grandma gave it to me, said it meant something, was important.
She wanted me to have it. She said she'd tell me the whole story
when I am old enough to understand. She always treating me like a baby.
She closes the window then continues, *I know it is my mom's.*
I know and I don't want it. I want to trade it in like she traded me in.
As soon as I pull into my driveway, she jumps out.
I get out and watch her walk to a telephone pole
where she comes face-to-face with her own face
smiling back at her.
She pulls the missing person sign down,
crumbles it up, looks back at me and says,
You know Crazy Kay, she came right up to me and Jolene on Broadway.
She asked if we had seen the girl on the poster and we just shook our heads.
She made us promise to keep our eyes out for her.
She laughs, then walks across the street
and onto her grandma's porch.
She hesitates, looks back, then opens the door and goes in.
I stand outside looking at the wind chimes dangling from Mary's porch.
Inside my daughter and husband are waiting
for the pizza I went out for and then forgot.

Light Pollution

Jolene calls a few hours after I ran into her—
she really wants my sewing machine.
She rattles on about my old restaurant family—
Rick left to work at the college cafeteria
because they offer better hours and benefits,
after Tommy found Edna dead,
he left his wife and now he and Maggie
go bowling every Sunday after their shift.
And oh, Maggie left Karl and Skinny Lynnie
got herself knocked up again,
her water broke during her shift.
Bob drove her to the hospital
wearing those ratty old slippers, you know
those slippers, he is still wearing them
even when it snows, he wears those slippers.
And he still orders the same damn thing,
Jolene says and together we say—
Two eggs over easy, burnt hash browns,
and whole wheat toast, lightly buttered.
I want to ask about Asif, but instead ask
for her address, so I can come over
and give her the sewing machine.
After I hang up, I walk outside
and look up, even though I know
stars are barely visible in the night sky
above our house on this one-way street,
maybe, just maybe, one is shining bright enough
through the city's light pollution.

Free

As our daughter spins around
showing my husband her new dance moves,
he notices her new haircut and says,
The back of her hair looks like
the blade of a guillotine.

I tell him how Chrissy offered to cut her hair
for free and how I felt bad saying no.
Nothing's free, Becky, he says, then adds,
now you have to pay to have someone fix it.
The truth is I paid her because she needed
the cash, but I will never admit this to him.

357 Prospect Street

After knocking for a few minutes,
a man donning an eye patch opens the door.
What the hell do you want? You look a little too old
to be selling Girl Scout cookies.
He moves out onto the porch and turns his head
and looks me over with his good eye
then keeps his eye on the sewing machine I'm holding.
I am looking for Jolene, I say.
He smirks. *Not too many ladies come here looking for Jolene. What'cha got there?*
I step back. *Is Jolene home?*
What'cha, a door-to-door seamstress?
I step back again. *Is Jolene home or not?*
He steps toward me. *Jolene don't live no wheres.*
As I turn, he moves toward me.
Hey, he says, *I got some pants that need mending.*
If you know what I mean.

Intimidation

On the next road over,
a group of five teens
walk slowly down the middle
of the road as my husband
inches his car forward.
One of the boys holds a bat
as if it's a club.
When the others move,
he stands there with his bat,
staring down my husband's car
as if it is a rival gang member,
only stepping aside when my husband
is a foot away.
What? he yells, thrusting his chest
at my husband's window, *What?*
Then the others yell and curse,
trying to intimidate a man
who just worked a double shift
to pay a mortgage for a house
in a neighborhood that he wishes
he could afford to move out of.

Angels and Sewing Needles

A few days after going to 357 Prospect,
Jolene calls around midnight,
Hey, sorry about that, I thought I'd be there.
I still want the sewing machine,
can you bring it by Hurricanes,
I am there every afternoon.
Can you come by this week?
I told my grandma about the sewing machine
and she is so excited, she says that
God must have looked out from behind
those clouds, saw her arthritic hands
and sent her an angel with a sewing machine.

Hurricanes

After walking into Hurricanes,
placing the sewing machine down on a bar stool
and sitting down next to it,
a ruddy-faced bartender comes over,
places a napkin down in front of me and says,
A woman walks into a bar with a sewing machine
and the bartender asks, What can I get for you?
and she says. . .
Vodka Martini, dirty, with extra olives, I say.
Alright, a Martini for you and what about your friend?
He asks, looking over the bar at the sewing machine.
Oh, nothing, she's driving.
He laughs, makes my drink and then sets it down,
still looking at the sewing machine.
I have to say this is a first, I have seen some bizarre things, but...
I interrupt, *It's for my friend, Jolene, who is supposed to meet me here.*
Jolene? You're friends with Jolene?
I nod and he shakes his head.
I hope you're going to sew her mouth shut with that.
I laugh.
You know I already 86'd her for the day. That doesn't necessarily mean
that she won't be back. She was in here earlier,
had five shots of tequila and fell off her stool.
After hearing Jolene's name, a few guys at the bar
start talking about how many times they've had her.
I look at them and one winks.
Behind them, I notice someone playing pool on the back table.
Can you watch her? I ask the bartender as I take my drink
and walk to the back.
I lean up against the wall and watch quietly. Wally the Whale,
an old customer at the pool hall I once owned with my husband,
knows I am there, but he just keeps shooting.
He's blocked all the pockets with plastic cups, so he doesn't
go broke playing. When he leans over to shoot, I notice
how cloudy his pupils have become and even though
he can't even see his shot, he still banks the seven in the side.

Where Mouths Run To

After running out his balls,
He asks, *How's your husband doing?*
I sure miss those real tables,
playing on bar tables after Crown Royals
is like going from driving a Cadillac
to riding a bicycle, he says
as he collects the balls from the cups.
And I think about how I miss
that hopeful feeling I had when
I was younger before reality rolled in
and dropped like your opponent's last ball.
The guy who winked at me comes over
and toys with Wally.
Wally, you going to play this gal?
Wally smiles as he racks,
Neh, you're gonna play her
and if she beats you, Jimmy,
you're buying me drinks,
and if you beat her, I will buy you drinks.
I know I can't back down and I know Wally
wouldn't bet if he knew he would lose;
he knows I am not all that great of a shot,
so this guy must really suck.
Jimmy starts running his mouth about
how no gal's going to beat him,
so I chalk up.

When Someone Wins

After I win,
Wally offers to pay for my drinks,
but I tell him I have to go.
You know, Jolene'll just pawn that sewing machine, right?
I nod because I know he is right,
but I will give it to her anyway
because I want to continue to believe
that people can change.
I want to ask Wally how his son is,
but I know he'll give me
that it-is-none-of-your-business look.
Tell your husband I said hi, he yells,
so the men at the bar stop looking.
They all poke fun of Jimmy, who hasn't
said a word since I dropped the eight ball
and Wally said, *Well, someone had to lose.*
As I pick up my sewing machine,
the bartender says, *Sew...,*
then dramatically pauses, before finishing,
glad you stopped by.

A Stick of Butter

Terry comes over for butter,
because Chrissy realized
she was short a stick mid-recipe.
Somehow he starts talking about
how unions are bankrupting the system,
how union bosses exploit workers,
how unions are ruining whole industries
and crushing the education system.
I try to argue the importance of
collective bargaining, striking,
and contracts. I tell him how
modern day robber barons
are intentionally using propaganda
to make the working class turn
on their own as he squeezes
the stick of butter in his hand.

Wrong Number

Around 2am, the phone rings.
Jolted from sleep,
my husband picks up.
On the other end,
a woman asks if he'd like some company
and my husband hangs up.
The phone rings again and I answer,
Who is this?
Becky.
Yes.
Oh. Becky?
Yes.
Hey, can I still get that sewing machine?
Jolene, it's 2am.
You can just leave it at Hurricanes.
I hang up.

Section 4: Do Not Enter

How Fragile We All Are

We are decorating Easter eggs
when we hear someone screaming:
STOP! STOP! STOP! PLEASE STOP!
From our porch, I see Patti suctioned onto
Henry's legs like a starfish.
In her window, I can see pastel eggs
hanging from the wilted branches
of their last Christmas tree together.
Since they don't see me,
I go back inside and close the door.
The eggs are soaking in a mixture of
food coloring, water and vinegar.
My daughter can't help lifting them
with a spoon to check their progress:
STOP! STOP! STOP! PLEASE STOP!
I echo, *They'll crack!*

How to Reattach Fallen Gutters

My husband helps Joe
put the gutter, that fell off his house
during the winter, back up.
He asks how his brother is holding up
as Joe climbs the ladder.
The waiting is the hardest part, he says,
the legal system is nothing like
an episode of Law and Order.
It has been well over a year
and they haven't even set a trial date.
My husband holds the gutter in place.
You know, you never think anything like this
could happen to your family
until it does, Joe says as he fastens
the gutter to the house.

Roller Skates

On my doorstep this morning,
I find a pair of used roller skates
three sizes too large for my daughter.
While she stuffs balled up socks into
the toes, so that her feet won't slip out,
I read the note from Crazy Kay:
Thought your little one would like these.
I am getting too old for roller derby.

After a Long Winter

Nina's outside raking up
all the dead leaves
the snow broke down
and Mary's picking up the piles
and putting them into bags.
They're laughing and singing
Ain't No Mountain High Enough
and Mr. Finelli, who is dragging
yard waste bags to the curb smiles
before turning around.

Bill and the guys drink beers
on their porch and have
bottle cap flinging contests.
They sing along with Nina and Mary.

Patti comes out to sit
on her front steps.
My daughter hula hoops
and Chrissy comes out and says,
That was one hell of a winter,
and I nod.

Then Sue comes out
on her crutches and
I walk over and ask
if she's having a boy or girl
and she says she likes surprises.

Patti walks up behind me and
says, *Honey, don't you worry,*
you'll have your fair share
of surprises in life, go find out!
as she sits down next to Sue
and places her hand on her belly.
Did you hear it is going to snow
tomorrow? No kidding, Patti says,
three to five inches.

The Crocuses

The crocuses rear their pretty heads,
dot city lots like hope.
Kay creeps up behind me as I admire
this transformation. She tosses
peanuts around for squirrels and
holds out the bag as an offering.
After I decline, she counters, *Suit yourself.*
Then takes out a peanut and places it
in her mouth, shell and all.
Then asks, *Did I tell you about the time*
Marty Weisenberg took me to the spring gala,
then ended up leaving with another girl?
That Weisenberg, what a jerk!
I think of him every spring
when the crocuses come up.
Kay bends over, picks a crocus,
pulls the petals back, exposing three stamen.
You see, just like this flower,
Weisenberg had three testicles.
She tucks the flower behind her ear,
reaches into the bag, pulls out
a handful of peanuts, some of which she
disperses and some she pops in her mouth.
Then she sashays away singing
Goodness Gracious Great Balls of Fire.

How to Haggle

My mother tells me her mother's body
is shutting down one organ at a time;
she wants me to drive one hundred
and ninety-three miles to say goodbye.

Since this is the third death warning this month,
we go ahead with our yard sale as planned.
Reluctantly, my husband drags boxes outside.

We place price tags on our past, spread memories
over makeshift plywood tables. I try not to think
about the order in which organs shutdown
as strangers rummage through our belongings.

An incredibly hairy man squeezes his bulbous feet
into my husband's old bowling shoes,
then limps around our yard, telling his wife
they fit just fine. The woman eyes the sewing machine

that I never did get to give to Jolene,
as her husband rolls a bowling ball into my flowers.
I want to ask them if it is true that
the heart and lungs really close down last,

but he offers me twenty bucks for the shoes,
the ball, one of my husband's paisley ties
and the sewing machine.
I say thirty and we agree on twenty-five.

His wife asks how much for a ceramic unicorn
with a chipped horn. *Just take it,* I say
and my husband gives me that smile
because he didn't want to waste his day this way

and he knows that if my grandmother dies
on the same day he takes a suspicious man
into our home to plug in a dusty DVD player
to prove that it works, he'll never hear the end of it.

What We Find, What Is Left Behind

Since Henry left,
Patti hasn't mentioned him
until today when
she checks her mail
as soon as
my daughter and I
get out of our car.
You would think that asshole
would get his filthy magazines
forwarded to his new whore's house,
she screams as she furiously waves
her mail in the air.
My daughter nonchalantly shrugs
as if just told there is only
vanilla ice cream left in the freezer.
This is what worries me,
how unresponsive we have become.
Once inside, I consider sparking a conversation,
but she is already unpacking her book bag,
unfolding a crumbled napkin, exposing
a dead wolf spider still intact.
Can you get my microscope? she asks
and I am grateful for her inquiry
and the opportunity to examine
the anatomy of a life
so much smaller than ours.

Invisible Snapdragons

For John Dorsey

I hold my daughter after
she wakes from a nightmare.
Angry cats were chasing us,
she says, *and you ran too fast.*

She puts her arms around my neck
and sobs. She is convinced
that the tapping on the window
is an army of cats clawing their way in,
so I push aside the curtains

and show her raindrops
piercing the murky night, but this
does not ease her fears, so I tell her
about flowers we will plant,

snapdragons, that she can
pop her fingers into like puppets,
how she can open and close
their dragon-like mouths,
but she wants one right now.

I tell her how as a kid,
I knelt beside my father
as he pushed seeds into the ground,
and he told me anything
worth believing takes time.

Until harvest, I had as little faith
in his words as she does mine.
Right now, the nightmare is vivid,
the rain is not retractable,
and she has never known
a flower that can breathe fire.

On the Rare Occasion I Get to See Her off to School

Last night's snowfall was unexpected
for mid-April
like an ex-lover
randomly calling after decades of distance.

I packed away our winter coats and gloves yesterday,
so my daughter shivers as we walk.
I have a doctor's appointment to see if we really are
expecting again.

In lieu of discussion,
we watch and listen to the city waking up.
Men slam the doors of their work trucks.
Women let their dogs out into their backyards.

By the dead end sign,
Crazy Kay is bundled up in a snowsuit
with a red plaid Elmer Fudd hat.
She's using a snow shovel
to clear the dusting of snow from her walkway.
When she see us she asks,
Can you believe this storm?

When we get to the bus stop,
a woman, pulling her son's hand,
so he won't dart into the road,
says, *I told that ho to back off,*
to another mother, who nods.

Terry pulls up in his work truck
to drop his kids off. He rolls down
his window and asks if
I can watch his kids this afternoon;
he got a side gig painting
for fifteen an hour, off the books.

My daughter inches away to pet
a woman's dog and when the bus comes,
she climbs aboard, without looking back,
and for some reason I feel empty,

so completely and totally empty.

The Portability of Love

For the first time this year,
I pull the lawn mower
out of the shed
to mow our tiny front yard.
While trying to start it,
I notice Nina sitting on her porch
talking on her cellphone.
When I was a teen,
phones attached to walls
and within earshot of the whole family,
I would stretch
the long spiraling cord
around the corner of our kitchen
and into the pantry,
where I would make secret plans
with boys while reading
the ingredients on the back of boxes
and cans. Now kids can carry love
around with them, answer anytime,
rub their fingers over keys,
text message or take selfies
to send when asked,
What are you wearing?
They don't have to worry
about their mother
holding a cup up against the door
or interrupting to retrieve
a jar of spaghetti sauce
or a can of creamed corn.

Two Down

After turning off the lawn mower,
I hear Sue calling me,
Becky, hey, Becky,
do you know a six letter word
for a group of birds,
it's not "flock" because it starts with a M.
I push the lawnmower to the shed
and walk toward the fence
that separates our yards.
Murder, I say.
Really? Sue asks,
That would be a better word
for a group of my relatives,
she laughs.
She is sitting on one plastic lawn chair
and using another to elevate her foot.
Gus, one of my regulars, does these religiously,
she says, holding up
a book of crossword puzzles.
He sent me these in the mail
along with a get well soon card.
Hey, did you work with Jolene? I ask.
Sue takes a pair of sunglasses
from her apron pocket
and puts them on.
You mean the Jolene who worked there
for three months,
made out with the entire kitchen staff
and two busboys,
who don't even speak English?
I nod, *Sounds like her.*

Working for the Man

Bill and his friends
are out on his porch
drinking beers
before noon
and talking about how
they are tired of
working for the man.
Bill yells to the one
who complains the most,
You don't even work, Brian.
There is silence for awhile
and then Brian responds,
Well, isn't that something?

Small Gifts

A new family moved into
the candy apple lady's house,
destroying our theory that the house
was turned into a grow house,
even though the front upstairs windows
are still boarded up.
The two little girls ride bikes
with our kids and we all sit
on Chrissy's porch, giving
the husband the low-down on the neighborhood,
while Bill tosses tiny plastic balls
that have bells inside of them to the kids.
You guys can have them,
Bill says, as he opens another can of beer
and slurps the foam off before adding,
my cat refuses to play with them.
The husband says thank you,
then steps on a conversational land mine
when he asks Bill how long he has lived here.
After about a half hour of Bill rambling on,
two skinned knees, one argument over cat balls,
and a close call with a blue sports car,
Bill asks, *What was the question again?*
And before the husband repeats himself,
Chrissy yells, *You answered it, Bill!*

The Thief

When Crazy Kay walks by
the kids pelt her with cat balls,
and we make them surrender their ammunition
to Bill, who forgot he even gave them the small gifts.
When Mary walks by and waves,
Terry, who has joined us, says to our new neighbor,
There goes the thief,
and Chrissy swats him and gives him that look.
Oh, come on, that woman is lucky she just got fired
and isn't doing time for stealing from old people, he adds
and Chrissy shrugs because the accusation sounds pretty bad
and these days people are guilty until proven innocent.

Just after Dark

My husband comes home
while we are still outside.
What I am making for dinner
hasn't even crossed my mind.

He walks over and says hi
and Terry asks him if he has noticed
the undercover parked a few house down.
My husband kicks a rock then says, *Yep.*
Terry adds, *Looks like the late night traffic
at Bill's is coming to an end.*

A few minutes later my husband
goes inside and then I follow,
mentally planning the menu
as I shove my daughter's bike
into the overstuffed shed:

angel hair pasta, olive oil, garlic
and whatever left-over veggies
I can throw in.

Umbrella and Birthday Cake

On our way home, my daughter and I
pick up an umbrella and cake
for my mother's 62nd birthday.

All day, I've been told, it looked
like the sad clouds wanted to grieve,
but I was stuck in a windowless room.

Now, we sit around the kitchen table
and chitchat about the recession,
my mother's friends who have lost

everything and will have to work
until they die just to pay interest on debt.
It wasn't supposed to be like this,

she says, sipping wine, we shouldn't
leave our children with less
than we had, she says and my daughter,

hearing the rain tapping at the window,
hands my mother the umbrella,
decorated with Van Gogh's Irises

and asks if it's time for cake.
We turn lights low, watch the candles
dance like red and orange irises: quivering,

twisting images that aren't meant to last.

Garbage Pie

The friend Terry was painting for
isn't answering his calls
and hasn't paid him what he is owed.
Terry keeps getting outbid for paving jobs
and Chrissy's baking job is
just not enough, so he delivers pizzas
three nights a week and tells me the
money isn't that bad and the stories are priceless.
Last week, I delivered to this old lady
who tried to pay me in pennies and nickles,
no joke. She had a glass bottle filled with change
and she wanted to count seventeen dollars
and eighty five cents in my cupped hands.
Then last night, I get to this house and
some dude answers in a chicken suit.

Crushed Lily

The crushed lily, cradled in my daughter's hands,
proves there's beauty in the folds of our faults.
She spreads back petals and examines the inside;
Focus, flip, then fold, as if a paper fortune teller,
or, as pre-teen girls call them, cootie catchers.
Ask me a question, I tell her, *pick a number, lift the flap.*

Where Is She Going, Anyway

Crazy Kay is walking down the street
wearing a red halter top and matching heels.
When she passes Bill's porch, the guys
whistle and Kay turns toward them
and yells, *She still has it,* talking about herself
in the third person. Bill raising his beer can
and yells back, *Sure do, Kay, sure do.*
After she is out of sight, Bill asks,
Where is going dressed like that before noon, anyway?

The Annuals

Even though Bill's wife
is long gone,
the annuals she planted
still come up to remind Bill
of what he has lost.
This afternoon after polishing off
a twelve pack,
he takes out his weed-whacker,
walks over to the flowers
and pauses there
with the blade hoovering
just above the petals.

Crazy like Bedlam or Sly like Fox

Terry tells me how Crazy Kay
ordered ten pizzas to the house
of the neighbors she has been feuding with.
When he realized what happened,
he knocked on her door, but she wouldn't answer.
He could see her peaking out through the curtains.

Shape of Stars

My daughter's finally asleep,
but I know if I get up
she'll call me back,
so I count her breaths,
the glow-in-the dark stars
stuck to her ceiling,
the number of dog barks
and sirens.

I think about Joe and Sue,
Terry and Chrissy,
the Finellis, Patti
and Henry, Maria, Nina,
and Bill, all the lies we
have all told and been told,
like how stars are pointed
instead of spherical.

Just Enough

Before the sun comes up,
the bread is in the oven.
Nothing has turned out
the way she planned, but
the smell of bread baking
and the way it rises like
the sun over the horizon is
just enough to make Chrissy
smile. Today she gets paid
and will have just enough
to pay for a portion of
her phone bill, just enough,
so service won't be disconnected.

The Verdict

Joe is outside in his driveway
working on his car.
Last week, after a plea bargain,
his brother was sentenced
to 25 years for manslaughter.
A picture of the woman
and the child he killed
made the front page
of the newspaper today
under the headline:
Has justice been served?
Joe doesn't know what to do
and he is tired of being punished
for a crime he didn't commit,
so he takes parts from
one broken down car in his yard
and transplants them into another.

Justice

Because she knows no boundaries,
Crazy Kay walks into Joe's driveway
while he is working on his car
and asks, *So do you think justice
has been served?* Joe looks up
from under the hood and asks,
Can you hand me that wrench over there?

The Practice Wedding Cake

Since Chrissy has been perfecting
sugar flowers for wedding cakes,
she comes over with a sample cake
and I put a pot of coffee on.
We let our kids chase the cats around
the house because we're both
too exhausted to tell them to stop.
I admire the cascading
            roses,
              violets,
                hibiscus,
                    and peonies,
while Chrissy tells me for the past two days,
Terry has been pissing blood and vomiting,
but won't go to the hospital because he has no
health insurance. Each tiny petal, leaf, stem,
all the intricate details of our lives,
our stories, our sacrifices, the way we come
together, with an empty plate, a knife and fork.

The Irises

Before orgasming with a man, I believed
Georgia O'Keeffe's Irises beautiful, light;
I considered white a color, not a lack of,
I knew nothing about art, about irises,
about the emptiness we spend our lives
trying to fill. I thought I was alone, one

flower on one canvas, spread like petals,
waiting. I never considered the difference
in perspective, Van Gogh's Irises in the wild
versus his irises cut in a vase on a table.
Is this how a man sees a woman? I masturbated

and felt shame. My mother caught me and
I couldn't look her in the eyes, they were
O'Keeffe's images before I knew of her paintings—
her haunting Black Irises, the center,
totally devoid of light or maybe all colors merged,
a feeling that can't be translated into just words.

Mistakes You Didn't Make

Sue's sitting beside her crutches
on Joe's front steps, engaged in a
crossword puzzle when I get home.
Hey, can you give me a lift
to the diner? Apparently there is
a paycheck there I never picked up.
Even though I have hours of grading
to do, I say, *Sure,* and within minutes
we are en-route.
I want to ask her why they didn't just
send it to her, but she is rambling on
about how Joe's mother's health
has gone downhill since her other son
was sentenced to 25 years in prison.
She has been staying
in bed all day, crocheting baby outfits.
When we get to the diner,
Sue tells me to drive around to the back.
She crutches in through an open door.
Outside are a row of upside-down
milk crates surrounded by
a carpet of cigarette butts.
About an hour later, after I finish
the crossword puzzle that Sue was
working on, she comes back out.
Her cheeks are puffy, damp and
speckled with evidence of grief.
On the drive home, I don't ask her
what's wrong and she doesn't tell me.
Instead she asks, *How many times*
do we have to tell her that
what happened is not her fault?
She opens her window.
I mean the outfits are just plain sad.
The stitches are

usually too tight or too loose.
Not one pair of three dozen booties
are the same size or shape,
one arm or leg of each jacket and pant suit
is about an inch longer than the other
and the hats are crocheted shut.

Heirlooms

After swimming at the Y, we find our locker open, my daughter's brooch gone.
We sit on the wooden bench, in our wet bathing suits, shivering, as I try
to explain how sometimes people take what doesn't belong to them.

Even though the damn thing was gaudy, nothing more than pieces
of oddly-shaped, painted glass glued onto a pot metal backing,
now that it is gone, its value has increased. What will happen when

she is older and loses what girls don't even realize is theirs? She
doesn't understand who could do something like this, so she starts
opening lockers in search of what is rightfully hers, the way I looked

into every man's eyes, wondering if he would return what I gave away
unknowingly. I should have used a better lock; the brooch belonged to
my great-grandmother. When she gave it to me, she confessed she wore it

in case she had to use the back to protect herself from frisky young men.

The Effort

The for sale sign
on the Finelli's lawn
will stay there for years
like Christmas lights left up
on the porches of
some of the other houses.
The listing price is
far above the worth
in this neighborhood,
but below the effort
poured in all those years
while everything around
crumbled. All that energy
wasted like trying to put
a sun in the sky
using spray paint.

Tears and Needles

A little after midnight,
the phone rings.
When I pick up,
Jolene asks if she can
swing by and pick up
the sewing machine
I said she could have.
When I explain that
I sold it at a yard sale,
she is silent for a minute,
then begins sobbing
and whines, *Everyone*
who I have ever loved
leaves me in the end.

How to Hail a Cab

In the library parking lot
a cab driver, about to pull out,
opens his window and shouts,
You certainly are a beautiful lady.

At sixteen, I would have
trembled awkwardly.
At twenty-one, I would have
liberated my middle finger.
At twenty-seven, I would have
looked around to see who
witnessed the driver's audacity.

But now at thirty-seven, I smile
and nod as I fish through my bag
in search of my library card.
The sun must be bright enough
to disguise the gray
and smooth my wrinkles;
for that, I am most thankful.

Counting down the Days

When I reach the speaker you order from at Burger King, Tony asks,
Do you want to try our new....

No, Tony, it's me, I just want my regular

Hey, Beck. Coffee, black, two ice cubes, so you can actually drink it before noon?

Yup, that's it.

When I pull up, he is smiling. *Hey, how are you? I haven't seen you in ages,* he asks and I am confused because he never asks.

What are you so happy about? I ask, before realizing how awful my question sounds.

Can't a middle-aged man who works at Burger King smile? And then he tells me he is getting engaged, and when I go to hand him exact change for the coffee, he says, *No, it is on me.*

When I say congratulations, he doesn't tell me how many days left of work he has; instead, he begins the countdown to his wedding day.

Surprise Party

The moving van in Joe's driveway lures the neighbors like crumbs do ants. Joe explains that he and Sue need a fresh start somewhere else, especially with the baby coming. He is renting out the house to his old employees and moving to Vermont. *Verrrr-mont?* Patti asks as if he said Saudi Arabia. *What are you going to do in Verrrr-mont?* While my husband, Terry, and Bill start to help the other guys load boxes and furniture, the rest throw together an impromptu party. Chrissy grabs one of the wedding cakes she has been practicing her decorating skills on and pipes out *We will miss you!* where the bride and groom would stand. Bill's boarders bring over beer and some beach chairs from Patti's backyard for people to sit on. The kids pick a bouquet of dandelions for Sue. Mary contributes potato chips and cans of cream soda. Nina tells Joe that she knows what it is like doing time with a loved one, then adds, *You can run away, but the pain will follow you no matter how far you go…,* and then gives him a big hug. Joe looks away from everyone when he says *thank you,* trying to conceal his tears. Mrs. Finelli, who I only really saw a few times, carries over a plate of crackers covered with cream cheese and capers. *What are these, sardines?* Patti asks, but no one responds. I get the baby bath towel, bathrobe and rubber duckie I picked up for Sue a month ago. Someone places a card table on my front lawn. This is how it happened, how we see Joe and Sue off into their new life on a Saturday afternoon on our one-way-street. Five minutes before they take off, Crazy Kay shows up with New Year's hats, noise makers and confetti that she passes out to everyone. Hours after they depart, after the street lights turn on and a police car drives by slowly, we are still out there, saying our goodbyes.

Independence

Just before Joe leaves, he puts a pile of stuff on the curb
with a "Free" sign. I spy a sewing machine and ask
if I can take it for a friend and he says, *Certainly,*
that was one of my mom's. He smiles as the people wishing
him good luck start rummaging through his junk.
Not long after Joe leaves, Patti asks some of the guys,
who live with Bill, to come over to her house.
A few minutes later, the men drag the skeleton of
a Christmas tree, adorned with little American flags,
out of her house and throw it on the curb,
alongside all the misery Joe is leaving behind.

Resilience

While sanding my front steps in preparation for painting,
Mary comes over smiling; she says she got her nursing home
job back. It's less about strength and more about resilience.

How'd that happen? I ask, as I sit down for a break.
*Well, Mrs. Harris died and left me that gold cross and
a letter apologizing for the story she made up about me.
I guess that black angel was looking out for me,* she laughed.

I look over at her wind chimes and think about how I saw Nina
that time in the pawn shop with the necklace, how I figured
Mary must be guilty, how quick I was to judge.

Crazy Kay comes up the street, pushing a cart filled with
empty bottles and cans that others are too lazy to return.
Hey ladies, she says, sitting down beside me, *Did I tell you
about the time I left my teeth on Bernie Drescol's bedside table,
and ended up finding them in his labrador retriever's mouth?
I had to wrestle that damn dog for hours to get my teeth back
and that Bernie Drescol slept through the whole ordeal.*

How to Hang a Hummingbird Feeder

For Annie Menebroker

Combine one part white granulated table sugar,
with four parts regular tap water, bring to a boil,
allow sugar to dissolve like existentialism into

metaphysics. Or would it be metaphysics into
existentialism? While it cools, look for a safe place,
by a window, to have your husband hang the feeder.

He will ask if you know that they are the only birds
that fly both forwards and backwards
and you will not answer. You will be busy

considering the possibility that this faux nectar
could attract something so exquisite, something
that you don't think could survive in this dismal

city. You will remember how your husband took
that dance class with you before your wedding,
how hard you laughed when the instructors

scolded you for leading and him for placing
his hands too low on your back. Now you are
looking out the kitchen window as he climbs up

a ladder to position the feeder. You tap the glass
and as you motion him to move a little left,
you realize what you are waiting for is already here.

167

Do Not Enter

When the motorcycle club shows up at Bill's house
traveling the wrong way down our one-way street,
the kids are in the front yard playing jump rope
and singing *Teddy Bear, Teddy Bear, turn around.*

Before they even get off their bikes, Patti warns,
Watch the kids, they are known to snatch them.
A minute later, Crazy Kay walks two of her dogs
up the street, passing by us without a word;
Fixated on the bikers, she walks into Bill's yard
and says, *Which one of you strapping young men*
wants to take an old lady for a spin? I love a man
who travels around with a ton of shiny metal
between his legs. The bikers laugh, even when one of
Kay's mutts lifts his leg and pisses on a motorcycle.

Alright, young lady, I'll take you for a spin around
the block, one of them offers. Patti's face turns
white as she watches Kay hand the dog leashes
to one of the other bikers, put on a helmet,
and climb onto the back of the man's Harley.
The new dog sitter, clad in leather, walks the dogs
over to where we are gawking, so the kids can pet them,
as Kay wraps her arms around the biker's waist,
rests her cupped hands over his groin and screams
If my momma could see me now! as he pulls onto the road,
and heads the wrong way up our one-way street.

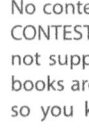

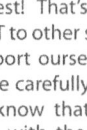

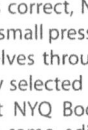

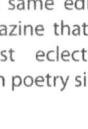

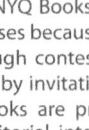

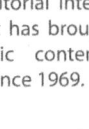

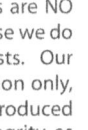

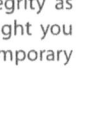

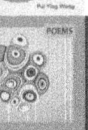

www.ingramcontent.com/pod-product-compliance
Lightning Source LLC
Chambersburg PA
CBHW022008080426
42733CB00007B/528